Jaylen Brown

Interesting parts you need to know
about Jaylen Brown

Brett L. Moyer

Table of contents

Chapter 1: Jaylen Brown Biography

Jaylen Marselles Brown was born on October 24, 1996. Brown presently plays for the Boston Celtics in the NBA. Brown grew up in Marietta, Georgia with his parents, Mechalle and Masreselles Brown, and brother, Quenton Brown.

Brown grew up as an extremely clever young guy, and some feared he was "too smart" to play in the NBA. This criticism was perceived as a racist prejudice towards African Americans. Brown is mostly a vegetarian, yet he has many broad hobbies. Some of his hobbies include studying Spanish, philosophy, meditation, and learning about history.

These hobbies speak eloquently of his brilliance. He attended Wheeler High School in Marietta, Georgia before departing for college. With both academics and basketball in mind, Brown opted to attend the University of California. Jaylen played one season with the Golden Bears before being taken 3rd overall in the 2016 NBA Draft by the Boston Celtics.

Jaylen Brown's Basketball Career
High School Career (Wheeler High School) (Wheeler High School)
Jaylen Brown attended high school in his hometown of Marietta, Georgia. He attended Wheeler High School. In his final year at Wheeler, Brown established his name on the map. He averaged 28 points and 12 rebounds each game while leading the team to a 30-3 record. Brown also helped Wheeler clinch the Class 6A State Championship that year by sinking two free throws with 0.6 seconds left. Brown's two free throws completed a 59-58 win.

This helped him gain a 5-Star recruit rating, establishing him as the 4th-best recruit in the class. Jaylen was selected as Gatorade Georgia Boys Player of the Year, USA Today's All-USA Georgia Player of the Year, and Georgia Mr. Basketball. He was also named to the McDonald's All-American Game.
College Career (University of California) (University of California)
The intellectual and athletic standout chose to leave his birthplace for the West Coast. On May 1, 2015, Jaylen Brown indicated that he would take his skills to the University of California, committing to the Golden Bears. While playing, he wanted to make sure he was still pushed intellectually.

In his single season with the Golden Bears, Brown totaled 14.6 points, 5.4 rebounds, and 2 assists per game. He played 34 total games for Cal. His career-high in college was 27 points, which he equaled twice. His 27-point performances occurred against Richmond on November 27, 2015, and against Utah on January 27, 2016. Brown was named First-Team All-Pac 12 and Pac-12 Freshman of the Year after a stellar season. After one season as a Golden Bear, Brown declared for the 2016 NBA Draft.

NBA Career

In the 2016 NBA Draft, Danny Ainge shocked several people by picking Jaylen Brown a few selections sooner than expected. The Celtics' bet has shown to pay off so far. Brown was taken third overall in the 2016 NBA Draft by the Boston Celtics. He officially finalized his rookie contract with the Celtics on July 27. His NBA debut occurred on October 26, when he scored nine points and blocked two shots. Brown's first career start came against the Cleveland Cavaliers on November 3, when he dropped 10 points. In his rookie season, he averaged 6.6 points, 2.8 rebounds, and 0.8 assists across 17.2 minutes of play per game. As a result, he was named to the NBA All-Rookie Second Team.

Brown showed enormous growth the following year, pouring in 25 points in the season opener on October 17, 2017, vs. the Cavaliers. He subsequently achieved his career-high of 32 points on April 6, 2018, in a victory against the Chicago Bulls. Brown was fast establishing that he had NBA scoring skills. He further established his claim by scoring 30 points against the Milwaukee Bucks in Game 2 of their first-round playoff clash. The 21-year-old became the youngest player in Boston Celtics history to score 30 or more points in a playoff game. He also added a 27-point game vs. the Cavaliers in the Easton Conference Finals that year. It did not finish where the Celtics hoped, but Brown showed tremendous potential early on.

The 2018-19 season began significantly slowly for Brown. Critics started to rise, as it looked like Brown was starting to fall in love with his jump shot instead of his customary slicing style of play. Brown did, however, come back from the early-season troubles and concluded the year with a season-high record of 30 points that he set against the San Antonio Spurs on December 31.

When it came time for the 2019-20 season, the Celtics needed to pay up to keep their budding star. The Boston Celtics elected to renew Brown on a $115 million contract that would keep him through the 2023-24 season.

So far, Brown has produced a respectable return on investment for the Celtics. On December 28, 2019, he equaled his career-high 34 points vs. the Cleveland Cavaliers. He is presently averaging 20.3 points per game this season.

Personal Life by Jaylen Brown
Jaylen grew up in Marietta, Georgia where he was born.
He was raised by his parents, Mechalle and Masreselles
Brown. He also has a sibling, Quenton Brown.
Brown grew up as an extremely educated guy, and has
frequently talked about the significance of education at
Harvard and MIT. Jaylen Brown is also known to be a
vegetarian. He is interested in learning Spanish,
philosophy, meditation, and studying history.
His father is a professional boxer and a member of the
Hawaii State Boxing Commission Board.

JAYLEN BROWN QUOTES
"Some individuals assume racism has gone or no longer
exists." But it's buried in more strategic places. "
"I'm emotionally and physically ready for anything."
"I had connected my life to basketball so completely that
it made me physically ill."
"Reading is looked at like it's cheesy or lame, but you'd
be shocked at what you can discover in a book."
"I don't have any fear of failing whatsoever. I used to,
and I promised myself I wouldn't let myself go anymore.
"

Chapter 2: How jaylen Brown started

Forsberg, Chris
Jaylen Brown wasn't doing a very good job of disguising his annoyance.
It was late in his first season and, although Brown doesn't recall precisely why he was unhappy, it seemed like a fairly safe bet to assume that a defensive error led to a fast hook from coach Brad Stevens. That left Brown stewing at the end of the Boston bench.

"My head was down or something," said Brown. "I don't believe it was because I was depressed or anything." But I wasn't playing, so I probably felt a little bit bummed.
recalling former Celtics strength and conditioning coach Bryan Doo: "Jaylen is sort of moping about and he's got that stoic expression that he gets when you can tell he's upset and you can tell he's frustrated." "Just sort of moving a lot sitting on the bench, and you can just tell because he's unhappy because he's not communicating with his teammates."

At that time, Doo's phone chimed. Thousands of miles away in his Malibu bunker, Kevin Garnett was wondering what was up with the rookie's body language. "KG watches a lot of games, remains a student of the game, and still observes everything." He texts me and says, "Yo, dude, what's up Jaylen? What's going on? What's wrong with his body language? He looks terrible, "remarked Doo. "Those are not all the words he used, but that was the idea of it, in the nicest terms," because I can't really recount precisely what he said.
"So I immediately texted him straight back and I was like, 'Yo, tough game. Brad grabbed him and he's struggling a little bit, he's fatigued. It's been a long year. But, sure, he's behaving right now. ' And (KG) was like, "Well, tell him I said this, and he began ripping off other stuff in my text..."

I replied, 'Kev, I gotta be honest, dude, it would mean a lot more to him if you simply gave him the message.' He's like, "I ain't calling, I'm not calling." So I told him, 'Leave me a message like what you just sent me and I'll simply play it for him.'
".... He left me a message and was just like, 'Yo, B-Doo, bro, tell Jaylen this is crap.' Going on and on about this or that. Then he was like, "Yo, tell him that you're in the big-boy league, you've got to strap up some day." It doesn't always go your way, but you've got to work out this or that. "

In a fitness area adjoining the Celtics locker room at TD Garden, Doo pressed his phone to Brown's ear after the game and instructed him to listen.
No, this is what the Celtics are about. Right now, pick your M-Fing head up.
Kevin Garnett in a voicemail to Jaylen Brown

"I can't speak all the words because there were a lot of swear words in them," said Brown, his cheeks lighting up when remembering Garnett's impromptu pep talk. "It certainly was cool for someone like him, who carried the Celtics heritage and safeguard the Celtics tradition when he was here, to come out to me.
I've admired him and his approach towards the game since forever. It was extremely encouraging and inspirational and impactful for him to come out to me and be like, "No, this is what the Celtics are about." Pick your M-Fing head up right now. "

It was also a stern reminder to Brown to control what he could manage. The No. 3 selection in the 2016 NBA Draft couldn't necessarily determine his playing time, but he could modify his mentality when things didn't go the way he wanted. He might have pushed the issue by bringing greater enthusiasm while he was on the court. It was a reminder that if Brown wanted to be as amazing as he imagined he could be, the route to greatness began with his mentality.

A GROWTH MINDSET?
This weekend, Brown will fly to his birthplace, Atlanta, to play in his first All-Star Game as a coach-voted reserve. The distinction is the result of five years of constant improvement and a tireless determination to improve regardless of the challenges in front of him.
Brown has so frequently grown as an NBA player that it's easy to forget exactly how raw he was entering as a 19-year-old after one season at Cal. Rewind the tape to his rookie season—the one that had him fuming on the bench—and it's amazing how much his game has improved.
Start with his playmaking. At the beginning of his NBA career, Brown struggled to throw even the simplest of passes and didn't see the floor effectively, particularly in transition.

Which is maybe why the most eye-catching figure in his advanced stat line this season is his assist percentage (the percentage of a team's field goals a player assists on while on the floor). He's at 20.2 percent this season, which is more than twice his career-best figure of 9.7 from last year and 9.9 for his career.
Point out the jump in Brown's assist rate and he shrugs. "My utilization rate is increasing, right?" he snaps back. Indeed, it has risen from a career-high of 24.7 last year to 30.5 this year.But a boost in use does not always translate into someone's assist rate increasing. In Orlando, fellow All-Star Nikola Vucevic's usage rate

made a comparable leap to Brown's this season —
increasing from 25.8 to 29.3 — yet his assist percentage
pushed up only 1.7 percent to 21.2. This year's figure
rises because Brown is so much better — and more
confident — at distributing the ball.

Brown's rise in assist percentage is also directly tied to
his better court vision. As a rookie, he operated with
blinders. He would rush into traffic with no strategy and
a poor ability to detect shooters or cutters. It resulted in
a shocking number of terrible turnovers, including a high
number of offensive fouls.
Brown now probes with confidence. He'll dance into a
thicket of defenders and know he can dump the ball
over the top to a big man. He attacks the paint with the
intent of spraying the ball out to shooters.
Even when he retains the ball, he's a different player.
Early in his career, Brown's handles were sometimes too
weak to reach where he wanted to go, and powerful
NBA defenders just wrenched the ball out of his hands.

Hours of dribbling workouts with assistant coach Tony
Dobbins have benefited Brown's improvement. Each
year, Brown appears to pinpoint a shortcoming and
make substantial progress.
The emergence of Jaylen the Playmaker
Brown's assist
0.94 turnover ratio as a rookie:
Brown's assist

This season's turnover ratio was 1.39.
This season, Brown is playing a lot more north-south basketball and bullies his way towards the rim with confidence. He had a bad tendency of attempting to make every aggressive drive into a poster dunk early in his career. Now he's content to bank home an easy layup after tip-toeing through traffic.

Just look at the contrast between Rookie Jaylen and All-Star Jaylen on these drives. For whistling, he would drop his shoulder and cross his fingers.Now he gets the 2020 Defensive Player of the Year in the air with a shoulder fake and beats him to the rim for a layup. This season, Brown is averaging a career-high 24.8 points per game while shooting 49.8 percent from the field and 38.9 percent from 3-point range.There was a time at the start of the season when it seemed like he would never miss a mid-range jumper again.

Free-throw percentage, which had been an obvious weakness in his game while shooting below 70% in each of his first three seasons, has risen to 78.1 percent this season.Hesitate after a technical foul and Brown will stroll straight to the line and take that shot. That's the type of confidence he's playing with now.
Former NBA All-Star Dominique Wilkins, an Atlanta great who has come to know the Georgia native better in recent years, understands that although booming

dunks frequently wind up in the highlights, it's the growth in other areas that converted Brown into an All-Star. "Now people are beginning to understand that this man is a complete basketball player," said Wilkins. "His game has evolved now. He's more mature now." You've seen the progress already, and it's going to do nothing but become better and better. "
"

The KG effect
When he watches games today, he doesn't simply concentrate on Brown's progress on the court. He regularly studies Brown's behavior in the huddles. The 24-year-old has come a long way from the guy who was sulking at the end of the bench as a rookie.
It's his confidence and his leadership to me. I see him engage with his teammates. That's what I watch, "remarked Doo. "I watch the sports, but I observe all those interactions." I observe the side bench things. To me, seeing him take the lead, make the handshakes, and how much he gives back to the team, whereas previously I'd seen him just sort of separate himself, was impressive.
"I know that he's confident in himself and his squad. And knowing Brad, how enthusiastic he is, how he's undoubtedly said to Jaylen behind the scenes, "You and Jayson, you're the future, right?" We need you to lead. ' Jaylen doesn't take such things lightly.

Once someone believes in Jaylen, I think Jaylen then feels he can go forward and achieve what he wants to do and is able to do. "
Doo said the message from KG wasn't really a light-switch moment for Brown. But it definitely connected with him at a moment when he needed a little harsh love and motivation.

Forsberg: Amid on-court success, Brown stays focused on off-court concerns.
"(KG) was very excellent at simply offering him advice in a non-'Hey, guy, I'm giving you advice' manner. In an aggressive but loving approach like, "Hey, dude, we're all in the league, we've all been here, you ain't no different than anyone else." "You're trying to make yourself different, but you ain't," remarked Doo.
"That's sort of the gist of everything. I know Jaylen truly enjoyed it. At the end, (KG) was more like, 'Also, you had skill, dude. You're going to be someplace, so keep pushing. ' It definitely mattered a lot.
Brown put in a lot of work and effort to develop his game to an All-Star level. But a little bit of KG motivation helped at the outset of that trip.

Brown said that as a rookie, "that gave me so much satisfaction in myself." "Like, yes, I could follow that too. This is one of the folks who has done something that I'm attempting to accomplish here...

Since then, it's given me a sense of what it's like to be a Celtic, as well as the culture and how deep the blood runs here.
It's his confidence and his leadership to me.

I see him engage with his teammates. That's what I watch, "remarked Doo. "I watch the sports, but I observe all those interactions." I observe the side bench things. To me, seeing him take the lead, make the handshakes, and how much he gives back to the team, whereas previously I'd seen him just sort of separate himself, was impressive.

"That's sort of the gist of everything. I know Jaylen truly enjoyed it. At the end, (KG) was more like, 'Also, you had skill, dude. You're going to be someplace, so keep pushing. ' It definitely mattered a lot.
Brown put in a lot of work and effort to develop his game to an All-Star level. But a little bit of KG motivation helped at the outset of that trip.

Brown said that as a rookie, "that gave me so much satisfaction in myself." "Like, yes, I could follow that too. This is one of the folks who has done something that I'm attempting to accomplish here...
Since then, it's given me a sense of what it's like to be a9 Celtic, as well as the culture and how deep the blood runs here.

Chapter 3: Jaylen Brown Aim in basketball

Jaylen Brown has a lot on his mind. In a picture studio in the southern suburbs of Boston, the NBA All-Star forward for the Celtics is oddly silent. Seeming much higher than 6 feet 6 inches, Brown's somber demeanor conflicts with his enormous physique. Ask him a question and what follows is a deliberate pause. This doesn't come across as a required habit of media training, but rather a sign that he's in continual deep contemplation.

Some journalists have misunderstood Brown's manner as stern or lifeless, yet a chat and a few hours of observation show numerous aspects to his nature.

On set with the photographer, Brown lazily spins a basketball on one finger, then grins for the camera with a variety of chameleonic faces, gaping his lips in pretended astonishment or stretching it into a goofy smile. He appears comfortable with members of his close entourage in tow.

"He simply has that spirit," adds his elder cousin Malcolm Durr, who acts as the creative director of Brown's fashion business, 7uice. "He sees something new—even if it's something he has no knowledge of—but if it captures his attention, he wants to learn about it, extract what he can and use it in his own life."

It's late morning in the middle of December, and the night before the shoot, the Celtics defeat the Milwaukee Bucks, the defending world champs. After missing five games in a row due to a strained hamstring, Brown returned to the lineup and scored 19 points. It's barely hours after the triumph, but Brown seems awake and calm.
It's the same winner's demeanor he's kept throughout his brief but significant career. When he was only 21, Brown became the youngest player in Celtics history to grab 30 points in a playoff game. Now at 25—and still a youthful, eager talent—Brown's strengths rest in his versatility and ability to keep getting better.

During the 2021 season opener for the Celtics, Brown poured in 46 points—setting a Celtics franchise record for points on an opening night— in a 138-134 double-overtime loss to the New York Knicks. As a player, he has a dominating presence on both offense and defense on the court.
Jaylen Brown was shot for The Red Bulletin on December 14, 2021.

Jaylen Brown
Jaylen Brown was shot for The Red Bulletin on December 14, 2021.

Off the court, his hobbies mirror the résumé of a great student with a comprehensive lineup of extracurricular activities. He's presently learning Spanish, engaging into meditation healing and studying history and philosophy. Soccer is his other sport of preference, and he considers himself an anime connoisseur and ardent chess player.

Brown played a year at the University of California, Berkeley before joining the Celtics as the third overall draft choice in 2016. But while he honed his skills in Boston, he was also developing more of a leadership position within and outside of the league. At 22, he became the youngest elected vice president of the National Basketball Players Association. He's an outspoken champion for the importance of education and technology, and he's engaged in high-profile talks about this issue at his alma mater, Harvard and MIT. Three years ago, he became an MIT Media Lab fellow, and since then, he's worked with the university to launch the Bridge Program, which mentors local high school kids of color who are intrigued about STEM.

And his own 7uice Foundation is geared towards revitalizing youngsters via sports, social and educational initiatives.
Although the NBA leadership has been more supportive of its players taking opinions on social problems than other major leagues in the U.S., Brown feels the next

level of action has to extend beyond demonstrations. He's seeking for more profound and real reforms throughout society that address structural disparities, particularly when it comes to education.

In a wide-ranging interview with The Red Bulletin, Brown glides from subject to topic with the oratorical ease of a professor, whether it's his exegesis on America's education issue, the dissection of his own mental-health journey or the weight of duty that comes with celebrity and power. It's a surprise shift for someone who's typically regarded as "too quiet." But his ability to interpret difficult ideas and convey them with clarity has the capacity to inspire conviction in what he's saying—and it's evident he hopes the next generation is listening.
Brown dribbles down court during a home game against the Atlanta Hawks on February 17, 2021. In the 2021 season opening in October, Brown finished the night with 46 points.

How would you characterize last year?
Jaylen Brown: If I could summarize 2021, two words spring to mind: "Love" is the first one, and the second one is "transformation."

Talk about the first word, "love."
In 2021, the sort of feeling I received is that if you were investing love into your work, into things that you wanted

to accomplish, into yourself, your neighborhood, your community, then I feel like you were receiving it back from the universe.

And transformation?

[In 2020], everything I was doing sort of got boosted. I had a career year. But also, I grew a lot. I felt like my frequency moved up a level, my knowledge, my clarity, things that had been right in front of me for ages, I began to perceive differently. My vision changed. I transitioned into the next phase. Transformation is important for me, and I think that's what [this past] year was.

You stated clarity about yourself. What would you think is one main misperception people have about you?
If I'm being honest, I have no clue what perceptions others have of me, and I could care less, too. I wonder what those items are. I've heard that I'm silent, particularly on the basketball court, I retain a straight-faced type of manner. People don't see me display a lot of emotions, so they assume, "He's intimidating," or "quiet" or "stoic." But the people who know me know I like to laugh, I like to grin, I like to dance, I like to tell jokes, I like to hear jokes, I want to make others happy.

Is it only close people who get to see that side of you?
Yeah, you can't show that with everybody. I'm a strong believer. But sometimes, this environment can be so

tiring. Sometimes I'm so focused on not letting somebody else affect me that I just kind of keep this normalized body temp, or I'm just the same for the most part because I'm trying to not let somebody else's BS rub off on me. I'm so focused on my own energy that I don't always share it or disseminate it the way I probably should. But I'm getting better at it. Maybe this year, 2022, I'll spread my light a lot more.

Do you believe people want to see you be more personal?
I'm not sure what people want to see. I'm still sort of figuring things out.

At any moment, Brown may be casually twirling a ball on his finger or articulating his views on the education situation in America.

What about fame? Have you achieved harmony between your personal life and being visible?

Yes, and no. I suppose I have strived to achieve balance between celebrity and personal life—and balancing all the other emotions and things that come along with it. For the most part, I believe I've done a decent job since I ain't nuts yet! A lot of people assume that because you're in the position you're in, there's no difficulty that comes with it. But regardless of your platform, regardless of who you are, every human has difficulty that they cope with to whatever amount. Nobody's exempt. You may be thinking somebody's circumstance is wonderful, but you have no clue what individuals are going through in their life. Balance is the term, trying to keep everything sort of in line. There are ups and downs. Sometimes, I become overwhelmed. Sometimes, you develop anxiousness and become stressed out. But I've found various methods to aid that process.

So frequently in our culture, they tell primarily people of color and young Black girls what they ought to dress, how they should have their hair. "You've had to wear a suit to be professional," "You've got to look and dress this way." Man, that's BS. That's conformity. And I don't agree. I'm not saying you should just go wild and have no form of structure whatsoever, but you're not going to remove my culture, you're not going to urge me to be more like you. That's not about to happen. Y'all get it through your skulls now. I ain't going.

Iverson was a zeitgeist of his time. What's been the greatest cultural difference for this age of players?
A lot more culture existed in the NBA back then. And a lot of stuff needs to be cleaned up because some of it was leading to violence. But today, you see this model that everybody's meant to be—how you're supposed to speak, how you're supposed to look, be politically correct, don't say anything controversial as an athlete or draw too much attention to yourself because you should have a fear of losing your sponsorships. I see so much more of it now. I feel like in this place that we live in

today, it isn't as encouraged to be your real self. It's a level: "You could be yourself.

I certainly want to see that transition where it's even more acceptable to be an athlete with a voice—an athlete who wants to do something else outside of sports, whether it's music, business, venture capital, fashion, whatever, for it to be appreciated. Yeah, it's our day job to play basketball, but we're also people. Y'all have a day job and y'all watch sports in your off-time. Some of y'all probably watch more sports than you do your work. For me, my day job, what I put a lot of work into, is playing basketball. But I also have other avenues. You attempting to tell me to shut up and dribble simply symbolizes society as a whole. I'll never shut up and dribble.

I want to be recognized as someone who shattered the mold.

Jaylen Brown
Are your other hobbies more intriguing to you than basketball?

No. I was born to play this game. I adore basketball. My mum would tell you I learned to walk by running after a ball. I felt like the ball selected me, I didn't choose the ball. Before I understood right or wrong, basketball was already my security blanket. Still to this day, despite all the BS and crap you go through during the sport, I enjoy this game in its whole. I can't image myself without it in my life. Basketball still thrills me like no other. And it reminds me when I get wounded, how much I adore this game.

But all the other stuff is intriguing as well. With education, it thrills my heart to watch youngsters start to break outside the box of what they tell you school is: "It's dull. It's not for you." There's so much more outside math, language arts, science and English. There's artificial intelligence, synthetic biology, DNA and RNA structures, and code. There are so many amazing things to learn about that you don't necessarily learn about going through school.

"You attempting to tell me to shut up and dribble simply symbolizes society as a whole. I'll never shut up and dribble," Brown adds.

Jaylen Brown
"I'll never shut up and dribble," Brown adds.

What do you believe is your best strength?
My biggest strength is growth. I believe I've proven it on the basketball court, where every year, I don't just become better, but my mindset evolves. And I believe that's where people get confused. They're like, "His talents became better." I've always had talents. You gain those talents, but it's only a set amount that you can continue to progress. This is a sport where if you weren't born with it, you ain't going to have it. You can't develop those things that God didn't place within you. I already

had talent, and through time, I've polished it. But what increased the most for me was my attitude and my approach, the development in my maturity, which enabled me to continue to do better in my work every single year.

How do you want to be remembered as a player and as a person?
As a player, I want to be known as a warrior, as a winner, competitive, tough. Obviously, a Hall of Famer. A legend. Somebody who broke the mold, transformed the culture, things of that kind. A champion. A pioneer.

Off the court? In the same manner, as creative, innovative, insightful, modest, loving. Somebody who helps make this planet a better place.

Chapter 4: Jaylen Brown Amazing facts

Cal swingman Jaylen Brown's draft status is fairly volatile right now. He is believed to be a lottery selection, although it is uncertain which pick he will be picked at. CBS Sports rates him as the fourth-best prospect, NBA Draft Net ranks him sixth, and Sports Illustrated puts him at eighth overall. He may land anywhere in the lottery.

While Brown's draft status may be in doubt, one thing that is not is his persona—which is much, much different from that of most basketball players. He took a grad school course as a freshman, rocked Asics, and was formerly captain of his middle school chess team. Yeah, hardly your normal NBA lottery choice. So, with this being the case,

Here are 13 Things You Didn't Know About Jaylen Brown.

1. He's a clever person.

A lot of prospective pro players don't take their education too seriously. Former Ohio State quarterback Cardale Jones notoriously tweeted, "We ain't come here to play school." "Classes are pointless. "

Brown, though, is a little bit different. He completed a graduate-level course in Cultural Studies of Sport in Education in the fall semester, learned to speak Spanish at a near-fluent level in his year in college, and intends to acquire three languages by the age of 25.

2. One assistant GM does not enjoy the fact that he's bright.

One NBA assistant general manager remarked, "[Brown] is an incredibly clever kid." "He took a graduate school class at Cal in his first year. He is a guy who is curious about everything. Because he is extremely brilliant, it could be scary for certain teams. He wants to know why you are doing something instead of simply doing it. I don't believe it's horrible, but it's a kind of challenging authority.

It's not malevolent. He simply wants to know what is going on. Old-school coaches don't want people who question things.

3. He's being tutored by Isiah Thomas and Shareef Abdur-Rahim.

Rather than engaging an agent, Thomas elected to depend on a set of mentors, which included NBA Hall of Famer Isiah Thomas and fellow Cal product and former NBA All-Star Shareef Abdur-Rahim.

Brown can only hope the advice Thomas is providing him is better than the advice he provided James Dolan when he was with the Knicks.

4. He was rated ahead of Ben Simmons as a high school prospect.

Brown was placed below Ben Simmons in both Rivals and ESPN's Class of 2015 prospect rankings, but Scout put him ahead of Simmons.

FC Barcelona is his favorite team.

Brown may be a basketball great, but his favorite team to watch plays on a pitch rather than a court. He roots for F.C. Barcelona in the Spanish soccer league, La Liga. Barcelona is home to soccer talents like Leo Messi, Neymar, and Luis Suarez. The team is a regular focus of Brown's tweets.

6. His favorite footwear is Asics. But they're about to be Adidas.

The majority of sneakerheads are infatuated with the newest arrivals from companies. Brown opts to go with Asics, or at least he did until he revealed that he actually signed with Adidas.

7. He was captain of his middle school chess team.

When you think of "Chess team captain," you probably think of a nerdy-looking person who couldn't run one circuit around the track without collapsing.

Brown destroyed this preconception when he served as captain of his middle school chess team. He continues to be a chess lover as he moves closer to the NBA. He attended a seminar on the game at Berkeley last year.

8. His mum nicknamed him "Old Man."

But the 19-year-old Brown is not like other youngsters his age. His passions include the aforementioned chess and table tennis. When he was given an Xbox as a present in high school, he gave it away since he doesn't even play video games. These tendencies caused his mum to call him "Old Man," owing to his propensity to behave like, well, an old man.

9. He's sort of a vegetarian.

Brown claims that the only time he eats meat is on road trips, since he didn't want preferential treatment from Cal's training staff. Outside of that, he abstains.

10. He plays the acoustic guitar.

During his time at Cal, Brown was more than just a beast on the court and in the classroom.He also took up playing the acoustic guitar—although he maintains he's no Jimi Hendrix.

I'm not going to toot my own horn. "I'm all right," Brown claimed of his guitar-playing talents to The Undefeated.

11. He's interned at a venture capital business.

While most NBA players stick to just one profession, Brown dives into another when he's not playing—the field of venture capital. He has interned at Base Venture, a California-based venture capital business. Erik Moore, who is a partner in the business, said Brown will continue to work there as long as he wants to. He also acknowledged his venture capital expertise.

In an interview with Scout.com, Moore said, "I can educate you on how to invest, and I can teach you how to be a venture capitalist, but I can't teach you the softer skills." "[Brown's] got it, instinctively and naturally." He'd be fantastic in this capacity. "

12. He's close with Bill Walton.

"He is one of the most intriguing, insightful, conscientious, and motivating people I've ever had the privilege to work with." And he's just 19 years old, "Walton told Ibabuzz.com." "His parents did a tremendous job, and his decision to come here to Berkeley, yeah, he's making the most of it. I could not be more proud. I could not be more enthusiastic about the future of the world. "

High praise coming from the best college basketball player in the history of the state of California.

13. He listens to Nickelback.
Accusing someone of listening to Nickelback has become one of the scariest charges you can throw at someone in 2016. It's borderline offensive. However, Jaylen Brown, however, does not feel it to be an insult. He has the audacity to boldly say he listens to the internet's least favorite band.